ALEXANDER "GREEK"
THOMSON
ARCHITECT 1817~1875

The aesthetic faculty appears to serve three purposes – the perceptive, the selective, the creative.

It is a matter of fact that the Greeks, who carried mental culture to a much higher degree than any other people, devoted their best energies to the study of aesthetics and to the development of the aesthetic faculty.

Alexander Thomson
Haldane Lecture, 1874

An exhibition in appreciation of the work of Alexander "Greek" Thomson on the occasion of The Festival of Architecture to celebrate the year of the 150th Anniversary of the founding of the Royal Institute of British Architects.

ACKNOWLEDGEMENTS

This catalogue has been published by the Architectural Association in conjunction with the Mackintosh School of Architecture and Third Eye Centre to coincide with the exhibition of original drawings by Alexander "Greek" Thomson together with photographs, models and modern drawings of his work. The exhibition is mounted at:

Third Eye Centre	Architectural Association
350 Sauchiehall Street	34-36 Bedford Square
Glasgow	London WC1
28 April to 24 May 1984	26 September to 27 October 1984

The exhibition 'Alexander "Greek" Thomson' has been assembled by the Graduate Department of the Mackintosh School of Architecture in conjunction with Third Eye Centre, Glasgow, who wish to thank the Royal Incorporation of Architects in Scotland for their encouragement, J. Fisher of the Glasgow Collection and the Mitchell Library, Glasgow, for the loan of material from their archives and, most importantly, the Scottish Arts Council for their financial support. Third Eye Centre is subsidised by the Scottish Arts Council and Glasgow District Council.

The following students produced drawings and models for the exhibition: Gill Malvenan, Gerry Grams, David Fleming, Ian Miller, William Alan, Alan Train, Kulwinder Panesar, Richard McAllistair, Alan Cooke, Robert Valentine, Mike Thomson, James Horne, David MacMillan (from the Mackintosh School of Architecture); Jan Nimmo, Rose McNight (from the Textile Department, Glasgow School of Art). Photographic work by Sim Beer (Mackintosh School of Architecture). Technical workshop Laurie Watson and Dick McLaren (Mackintosh School of Architecture).

The Architectural Association wishes to acknowledge the substantial efforts and meticulous recreation of "Greek" Thomson material by the Mackintosh School of Architecture – Mark Baines, exhibition organiser and compiler of catalogue material, Tony Vogt and Professor Andy MacMillan – and Third Eye Centre – Mike Tooby and Nicola White – in the production of this exhibition. Catalogue produced for AA Publications through the office of the Chairman, Alvin Boyarsky, assisted by Micki Hawkes, and the Communications Unit, coordinator Dennis Crompton. Catalogue designed by Dennis Crompton, production editor June McGowan, photographic reproduction by Sim Beer, John Gilmour (The Ideal Format) and Paul Barnett, photosetting by Charlotte Coudrille, Marilyn Sparrow and Angela Zammataro. AA exhibition by Amanda Innes.

Printed in London by Spin Offset Ltd
© The Architectural Association 1984   ISBN 0 904503 52 6

CONTENTS

Front cover:
Detail of the Cairney Building

Back cover:
Cartoon by David MacMillan, March 1984

Below:
Design for Monumental Building (*Project*)
A monumental composition with elements
of Thomson's previous Caledonia Road
Church, but prefiguring his later Queen's
Park Church.

A. Thomson, CALEDONIA ROAD CHURCH, Hutchesontown, Glasgow.

Foreword

Local Heroes: International Figures?

The world of architecture in Glasgow has been bestridden in recent years by Mackintosh, a colossus whose blinding light and giant stature have obscured talents only a little less worthy of international interest and repute than his own.

This exhibition and catalogue seek to redress the balance a little in respect of one such talent at least, Alexander "Greek" Thomson, an immediate predecessor and long-admired local hero whose works have now been catalogued and brought to public notice in McFadzean's long-awaited book.

The exhibition is intended to convey the power of his architectural imagery and the intellectual quality of his intentions in a more concentrated way through the use of original drawings extended by measured studies and models executed by students of the Mackintosh School of Architecture, while the catalogue essays attempt to identify his place in the development of architecture and to appraise his achievements in a time of great change and innovation in building and society.

The essays concentrate on a particular aspect of Thomson's work, his exploration and development of the serial urban facade, which paradoxically he examined as much through the unique occasion of the churches as the reiterated examples of the linear tenements, be they domestic or commercial. They also tend to accept without overt interest that late nineteenth-century Glasgow was the locus of major architectural energy and innovation, a characteristic shared with other provincial centres like Barcelona and Chicago, where major figures and complementary schools have already been identified and documented.

The essays all engage with the idea of the architectural role of the facade, whether as a weightless screen from the exterior (Baines), or as a 'wall of light' from the interior (McKean), or a problem of serial repetition (MacMillan). Their rejection of the hung-up canons of recent criticism concerned with 'programmatic need', or 'social justification' and their return to the assessment of performance at an architectural level, are a welcome augury of future discovery and criticism.

It is hoped that this exhibition offered by the Third Eye Gallery, the Mackintosh School of Architecture and the Architectural Association, London in the Festival of Architecture year will excite further discovery and enjoyment of "Greek" Thomson.

Andy MacMillan
Prof. Mackintosh School of Architecture
March 1984

Alexander "Greek" Thomson

BIOGRAPHY

Alexander Thomson was born on 9 April 1817, the seventeenth child of a book-keeper, in Balfron, some fifteen miles north of Glasgow. Following the deaths of his father and mother, between 1828 and 1830, he moved to Hangishaw on the southern outskirts of Glasgow and lived with his elder brother William, a well-educated scholar of Classical and Ancient languages. A chance meeting with the Glaswegian architect, Robert Foote, in 1834 led him to leave the lawyer's office where he had worked from the age of twelve to train as an apprentice architect. By all accounts Foote, though not an outstanding practising architect, proved to be an inspirational teacher, giving the young Thomson a thorough grounding in the principles and ideals of Classical architecture.

Following Foote's retirement in 1836, Thomson joined the firm of John Baird, eventually rising to the position of chief draughtsman, primarily responsible for the production of construction drawings, and the supervision and administration of contracts.

His marriage in 1847 to Jane Nicholson, the daughter of the London architect Michael Angelo Nicholson and grand-daughter of architect/writer Peter Nicholson (responsible for laying out Carlton Place in Glasgow) introduced him to her brother-in-law, John Baird (a young Glasgow architect unrelated to the elder Baird) with whom he joined in partnership in 1849. This partnership produced a series of villas and the Caledonia Road Church and lasted until 1856 when, through mutual agreement, it was dissolved and Thomson, with his brother George, established the firm of A&G Thomson, their first commission being the Double Villa at Langside.

In addition to the volume of work undertaken by the practice, including some speculative ventures of his own – the Grosvenor Building, Moray Place (where he subsequently lived), and Great Western Terrace among them – Thomson was also a founder member of the Glasgow Architectural Society (1858) and later of the Glasgow Institute of Architects (1868) and was president of both in 1861-62 and 1870 respectively. Thomson's enthusiasm and active commitment to these organisations earned him a great deal of respect among his fellow architects to whom he presented a number of papers concerning art and architecture, culminating in the series of lectures given to the Haldane Institute in Glasgow in 1874. Robert Turnbull joined Alexander Thomson in 1873, two years after his brother, George Thomson, left for Africa and until 1883 carried on the work left after Thomson's death.

John Baird, his former partner and then President of the Glasgow Institute of Architects, described the event thus:

. . . It was unanimously resolved that it be recorded in the minutes of the Institute that Mr Alexander Thomson died on 22 March 1875, universally regretted by his fellows by whom he was held in the highest esteem as an architect of Genius and an amiable and honourable man. . . He ever took a lively interest in its (the institute's) prosperity as well as in all other matters affecting the architectural profession, and he was especially zealous and persevering in promoting the education of young men and in encouraging their efforts and aspirations towards that higher artistic excellence which he himself so steadily kept in view and so successfully pursued.

"GREEK" THOMSON, CHARLES RENNIE MACKINTOSH AND FRANK LLOYD WRIGHT

Andy MacMillan

Glasgow and Chicago underwent their main development in the latter half of the last century. Both cities were the scene of great architectural ferment and activity; the new inventions – gas, electricity, cast-iron, plate glass, lifts, etc. – were in the process of incorporation into the new bigger buildings which the prosperity of the age demanded. Belief in the causal nature of architecture is reinforced on finding the same discoveries independently arrived at, in the same context, on both sides of the Atlantic.

This emerges clearly in the works of Thomson, Mackintosh and Wright. Thomson in the eighteen sixties and seventies and Mackintosh in the eighties, nineties and first decade of the twentieth century were investigating different aspects of the field which Wright was to synthesise from 1890 onwards.

Thomson is an architect's architect, admired for his invention, his precise controlled style, his great romantic city churches and for his ornament which is trivial and mechanical. His real significance lies in his development of the continuous building, the tenement and the office/warehouse and in his anticipation, by at least twenty years, of the work of Wright.

In the field of the continuous building, his basic discoveries appear almost immediately in Walmer Crescent, where the powerful horizontal trabeated upper storey unifies the entire block and the squat

Alexander Thomson, HOLMWOOD, Cathcart, Glasgow, 1857.

geometric projections of the bays articulate the subtly modelled, rusticated lower stories. He continued to study a variety of linking and articulating devices in a prodigious output of tenement facades over the next few years, from the over-ornamented Eglinton Street block to the more relaxed and powerful buildings at Queen's Cross and Park Road. The backs show that as yet the visual preoccupation is only facade deep, or perhaps more fairly, that Thomson is working in the field of street architecture.

His Egyptian Halls display the penultimate[1] Victorian response to the problems of the glazed office wall. Deeply modelled, intended to be viewed obliquely from the street, defined between a massive cornice and a strong podium, the intervening storeys are fully trabeated and stand visually in front of the glazing. On the upper floor the glazed screen 'weather' wall is actually set back clear of the loadbearing columns; a device which appears from time to time in his domestic work.

The small-scale terraces in Strathbungo and Hillhead provide a visual link between the two aspects of Thomson's contribution. On the one hand, they demonstrate a most skilful solution to the problem of the anonymous terrace, i.e. where the individual units are not identified, and on the other hand, in scale, rhythm and in the overtones of the Greek *stoa* they speak to Wright's early works like the Hillside School and the Riverside Golf Club.

The Mansions at Holmwood, Langside and Uddingston with their horizontal lines, low, sweeping roofs and general air of organic unity and being built in the round, presage the later discoveries of Wright's Prairie houses. They share the same geometric articulation, the same use of horizontal regulators at door height inside and the incorporation of outhouses and service buildings into a single building mass, the same integration of houses and garden by die-walls, steps and terraces.

Frank Lloyd Wright, W.E. MARTIN HOUSE, Oak Park, Chicago, 1903.

His major churches are reminiscent of the Mayan 'block' houses of the twenties and display similar aggressive geometric surface qualities and interest in scale, while the Ballater Street Church speaks externally to Unity Chapel.

Thus aside from their common awareness of Greek architecture, Thomson and Wright share an interest in the plastic organisation of wall surfaces, interpenetration in geometrical volume, articulation in architecture in the round and in the integration of nature and the building.

Wright and Mackintosh are contemporaries; Wright is consciously less historic but both men stand together in their manipulation of light and space, in their interest in the nature of material, in their appreciation of the art of Japan and particularly in their furniture designs.

Where Thomson's buildings contained their space behind a disciplined classic facade, Mackintosh rediscovered the capacity of vernacular building to allow free expression of its inner space, even to the extent of allowing it to penetrate through the outer face, as demonstrated in the Hillside houses. In addition to

Charles Rennie Mackintosh,
GLASGOW SCHOOL OF ART, 1907.

inventing a non-historic style of ornament, freer and more abstract than that of Sullivan, and more dependent on the exploitation of the materials involved, he discovered and explored the same concepts of continuous interpenetrating space and of organic unity of concept and detail as Wright. The life modelling room of the Glasgow School of Art is the most truly Wrightian space in Europe.

Mackintosh also, via his interest in vernacular building and in Japanese art, rediscovered the value of natural materials and in this sense the School of Art is the first Brutalist Building, Brutalist in its conscious exploitation of the potential of both material and structure and in the manner of its circulation space.

1.   The ultimate Victorian solution was the cast-iron facade superbly exemplified by Gardners' Warehouse in Jamaica Street, Glasgow.

Previously published in the Glasgow Institute of Architects' *Year Book*, 1967.

Form, Facade and Rhythm

Mark Baines

It is the intention of this essay neither to describe nor document the full extent of Alexander Thomson's undoubted, though neglected, architectural achievement but to concentrate on a specific aspect of his work – the development of the urban facade – identified as deserving the most critical attention, and in the process touch on those aspects of lesser-lasting significance by referring to them only as they serve to illustrate this central theme. The origins of its development, and progressive refinement, can be attributed to a number of influential and perhaps fortuitous factors initially involving an examination of two disciplines, the first broadly contextual, the second self-imposed.

CONTEXT

The near-unprecedented pace and extent of commercial development in Victorian Glasgow provided the necessary stimulus, demand and opportunity for original and inventive thought in all fields of human activity, including architecture, which had to adapt itself rapidly to meet not only changing programmatic requirements of buildings, but also the social, cultural and economic aspirations of an emergent urban middle class whose varied ambitions and wealth became the primary source of architectural and artistic patronage. As an architect, Thomson was deeply involved in the cultural and professional life of the expanding city, its robust and dynamic character leaving an indelible impression on the formative mind of the young architect.

With the exception of his villas, the vast majority of his buildings are set within central Glasgow, and are therefore subject to its largely predetermined urban context of gridded street pattern, plot and building line, which to some degree dictates the building's overall dimensions and organisation with respect to entry, servicing, front and back – accepted traditional relationships within which he generally worked, thereby absolving himself from any innovation in this respect. The nature of the commissions he received represented a limited range of building types, including the domestic – villa, terrace and tenement; the public – church; and the commercial – office and warehouse: all reasonably modest in scope and scale, and for which some established precedent already existed. Significant among these types are those of a commercial or speculative nature (terrace, tenement, office and warehouse) reducing the architect's freedom of expression of an individual's requirements, and resulting in a tendency towards an equalisation of space and amenity in a building of multiple occupancy.

Consequently the recurring similarity of accommodation within each type led to easy familiarity with their functional requirements, freeing Thomson to engage in the problems of their formal expression through the manipulation of volume, mass and, in particular, the detailed articulation of the enclosing fabric.

The marked similarity of both context and type links the scale and nature of his successive projects allowing like to be compared with like, more or less directly, as a painter may compare one canvas with another of the same complexity, size and subject.

To this end every successive commission served as the means to develop and experiment with these progressively singular and personal preoccupations, encouraging their constant refinement and elaboration – one building being prototypical of another of its type and engendering in turn a corresponding cross-fertilisation of ideas among the various types.

SOURCES

The second discipline is that of architectural style.

As his posthumously appointed title "Greek" suggests, Thomson's primary source of inspiration was empirically founded on the basic formal and structural principles and components of Greek architecture – podium, column, lintel, wall and roof – an essentially simple structural and material discipline, which through the application of sophisticated proportional geometry achieved a monumental presence.

To Thomson this purity of form and structure represented the root source of a civilised architecture and therefore an appropriate point of departure for his own work – a powerful and tangible image which he sought to transpose to his own era and impose on all his buildings.

However, the substantially iconographical role of the temple in Greek culture naturally did not equip it to deal with the complexities of spatial organisation and environmental control required of a nineteenth-century building. Rejecting the inevitable folly of archaeological reconstruction and the consequent burden of an academic classical dogma, he eschewed historical accuracy and instead embraced its principles and attempted to apply them with an intellectual detachment uncharacteristic of his contemporaries. In addition he selectively drew on architectural forms from Phoenician, Attic, Assyrian, Egyptian and Romanesque cultures in order to augment and enrich his palette and deal with those problems for which Greek architecture offered no precedent.

Thomson was therefore forcibly engaged with the twin dilemma of preserving the original innocence and potency of the chosen architectural image whilst coping with the increasing burden of technical performance of the building enclosure, and it is a measure of his genius that his buildings preserve the strength of the original aesthetic intention from conception, through development to their ultimate realisation.

COMPOSITION

The composition and massing of Thomson's buildings attempted to achieve a totality of form which was three-dimensionally definitive and therefore incapable of further extension. To this end several organisational devices were employed which formally established and exploited the existence of a building's geography in order to determine the limits of its physical extent.

Perhaps inevitably, symmetry of either part or whole was the primary generator governing either the individual parts or the whole of a building's organisation, resulting in two distinct compositional types. The first is characterised in his villa and church designs by an asymmetric whole comprising symmetrical components representing the principle volumes contained within the building and receiving an equivalent expression externally. The second is a symmetrical whole comprising asymmetric but repetitive parts with localised expression of the principle volumes or events as apparent in his tenement, terrace and commercial buildings.

Both configurations arise through manipulation of a series of independent formal elements, more or less related to internal function and linked by means of implied intersection or penetration – an implosion of pure forms – bound together by an all-enveloping surface texture conspiring to create the effect of monolithic construction as if the major elements of the building had been hewn from single solid masses.

The solidity extends to the building's base which is consistently recognised either through differentiating the surface of the stonework or more complexly by manipulation of the ground, setting the whole composition or superstructure on a horizontal plane to accommodate any variation in ground level, giving the building a more expansive monumentality setting it firmly and unequivocally in its topographical context.

A marked preference for the tripartite disposition of elements formally reflects the underlying symmetry which, depending upon context and building type, received greater or lesser emphasis, indicative of the relative autonomy and independence of the building as a whole. Thus, while a freestanding terrace received pronounced projectory end bays (Moray Place), a commercial building may only display minor end pediments at parapet level (Grosvenor Building) in recognition of the latter building's position within a continuous street frontage.

The placement of entry at once establishes both major and minor axes resulting in the almost inevitable frontality displayed in his buildings as well as complementary hierarchical relationships between adjoining facades of the building. One physically determines another, the whole reflecting and reinforcing a corresponding hierarchical structure in the surrounding orthogonal street pattern. The resultant isolation of each facade or wall, though substantially predetermined formally, became relatively autonomous and therefore capable and deserving of independent organisation.

The rhythmic description of the facade's vertical and horizontal dimensions became the object of seemingly inexhaustible fascination for Thomson.

THE FACADE

The facade's development from inanimate flat surface to a vibrant three-dimensional dialogue between solid and void, found embryonic expression in his villas and reached ultimate sophistication in his later commercial buildings.

The role of the villa in this respect is crucial in that it allowed Thomson to conduct small-scale, localised experiments with solid/void relationships which were extended in his larger-scale projects. The physical distance separating windows was gradually reduced to produce closer groupings of openings which, taken together, read as one window subdivided into separate openings. Further reduction of the separating mass of the intervening wall produced the colonnaded screen with windows arranged in series, leading to the partial, and ultimately to the total, detachment of the window frame from the masonry screen (Double Villa).

In general terms the terraced facade was transformed into a series of receding planes, vertically stacked and more or less related to floor level, each individually modelled according to its relative position above ground level. The greater proportion of the mass was concentrated towards the ground whilst the roof pediment or eaves achieved near total independence (Moray Place, Northpark Terrace) carried with the minimum of support.

In determining the metre of the rhythm achieved through the spacing of solid and void along the length of a facade, simultaneous consideration had to be given to both internal and external requirements of scale, function and proportion.

Thomson constantly sought to impose a regular spacing of openings along a building's length, reflecting the similarity or continuity of the internal space by suppressing, as far as possible, any significant evidence of its actual (domestic) or possible (commercial) subdivision (Moray Place and Egyptian Halls).

Such evidence as was given manifests itself through attached entry porticos or the appearance of chimney stacks at roof level, helping to create an intermediate rhythm punctuating the overall composition.

His progressive reduction of the solid/void interval along a building's length gradually eroded the wall's physical mass to such a degree that it adopted the role of a structural frame or screen. Generally a more relaxed rhythmic pace was given to the domestic building, whereas a commercial building displayed a more intense rhythm. Inventive exploration of the depth of the wall between openings through a series of precise incisions exposed an underlying structure buried behind its superficial anonymity. The intervening masonry was subsequently relegated to a recessed plane and thereby acknowledged as construction skin contained between points of support, encouraging the implication that it should read as void, becoming rhythmically engaged, like its glazed counterpart, through light and shadow (Northpark Terrace, Moray Place). Through equalisation of the dimensional relationships of solid to void – actual or implied – attention is directed almost equally to both, encouraging the eye to constantly move across the whole extent of the facade.

Such structural orchestration of the wall had the corresponding effect of producing a continuous band of masonry reading as both lintel and base, supporting (or supported by) a colonnaded band of windows giving the impression of a seemingly inexorable horizontal thrust, demanding containment but with the potential of infinite extension. In the absence of any projecting end bay this was terminated either by dropping the lintel on the same plane without any visual articulation to create an all-enclosing frame, or by a simple return to imply the existence of a corner (Egyptian Halls).

Such emphatic horizontality and linear continuity, achieved through the distinctly independent detailed articulation of each level, was appropriately expressive of the spatial organisation of the terrace, linking as it does volumes of the same dimension and function. The bilateral spatial distribution of volumes characteristic of tenement and commercial buildings logically justified an equivalent articulation of the facade, simultaneously expressive of both linear and vertical continuity. In contrast to the relative freedom of action that operated in determining a linear rhythm, the physical constraints imposed by intervening floor levels of equal height warranted the apparent detachment of the wall from their controlling and potentially divisive influence. This relaxation of the wall's reliance on the floor level achieved a radical transformation of the facade's overall proportions, suggesting at its most extreme the superimposition of two scales – internal and external – almost separate and contradictory in their new-found independence.

This relates particularly to the aforementioned speculative building which consistèd of a base and three upper levels of equal height, on which Thomson overlaid the classically-inspired tripartite division of the facade consisting of base, piano nobile and attic, each identified by a slight recession in the plane of the wall, each carried through to the next by attached aedicules to the first floor level windows, and by means of a continuous but stepped band to accommodate the window openings of the intermediate level (Queen's Park Terrace, Cairney Building). The merging and interlocking of successive levels eased the visual transition between the upper and lower parts of the building and obscured the precise junction of the floor and inner face of the wall. By virtue of the pronounced verticality Thomson was able to maintain and positively accentuate the linear rhythm. The vitality and visual intensity of Thomson's facades executed in this manner gives the impression of having been carved in low relief, with an illusion of great depth and layering suggested by the way in which one plane appears to rise from behind the one below, its profile 'silhouetted' against the one above. The implied stepping of the wall suddenly became reality as the timber clerestory became partially, then completely detached from the masonry frame (Grecian Chambers, Cairney Building), contributing to an overall lightness of effect, each plane and its constituent parts structurally independent of another for its support.

Dismissing previous experiments involving the apparent futility of placing a traditional structural order over a transparent base of shop frontages, Thomson strove to curtail the inevitable gravitational thrust of the building towards the ground by suggesting instead that the wall was an assembly of a set of components hung as a screen on a larger structural frame. Evidence of this idea is supported by the repetition of a limited number of elements of such a scale, proportion and jointing that they could readily be adapted to prefabrication or moulding – a step which prefigured the ultimately large-scale developments in cast-iron, and later, steel, of the curtain wall and framed structures in Europe and America.

Decoration in this context was only used where an intensification of the surface texture was required to denote or accentuate events on the facade such as a change in plane, base or top, or to give continuity to a series of elements. The decoration therefore helped to describe the building's facade as a series of individual parts or elements bound together by means of an all-embracing, single material finish. Consequently, the exteriors of his buildings have an abstract quality wherein each element is devoid of any expression of the material of which it is made, or how they are put together, suggesting a determined attitude towards materials in which the means and process of construction were not the major determinants of a building's form but were themselves chosen on the basis of the primary formal considerations. Stone, timber and glass are often consequently stretched to the limits of their structural capabilities. Constructional details were intended to support the overall architectural intent and were evolved as part of a continuous process of physical reduction and simplification to maintain a building's purity and monumentality – qualities which are essential to the Greek aesthetic – without interference of extraneous accretions of insignificant detail which would have inevitably trivialised a building's outward integrity. Hence the hidden or secret gutter avoiding external downpipes, concealed or detached window frames, the use of large areas of plate-glass (a new material) or the remarkable feat of fixing translucent glazing directly into masonry openings (St Vincent Street Church), the latter representing the ultimate achievement in this respect. It was the detail of effect rather than the pragmatic aesthetic of the craftsman.

Ultimately for Alexander Thomson the development of a highly personal architectural philosophy coupled with a conspicuous absence of any major public commission – an event which would have immediately thrust him to the forefront of the public eye – contrived to restrict the scope and scale of any potential impact of his buildings within the broad spectrum of architectural history. His intellectual determinism, derived from the essence of Greek architecture, was a point of departure from which he developed an artistic discipline corresponding to personal identification with a set of architectural values appropriately expressive of, and sympathetic to, his epoch. The abstract translation of these principles across time and the consistent maintenance of their essential spirit and dignity through inventive and sensitive contextual reinterpretation was achieved without evading the inevitable but necessary reality of the confrontation of the ideal with the practical.

Alexander "Greek" Thomson is therefore identified as a master of architectural metaphor, a creative and uncompromising architect capable of transcending transitory values, one whose architecture embodies a unique and indivisible fusion of the historical, the contemporary and the visionary.

Moray Place

Two storey terrace, terminated by projecting end bays with full height order of pilasters. A regular spacing of windows and entrance doors is set within a solid base, supporting a continuous colonnaded screen, the party-wall junction suppressed by use of a recessed solid plane.

Northpark Terrace

Restrained layered facade, the
upper colonnaded order con-
taining an alternating pattern
of wall and window.

Queen's Park Terrace

The tripartite division of the wall as applied to a tenement: ground floor shops, attached aedicules to first floor windows, stepped section over second floor windows with partially colonnaded third floor, the recesses between columns intended to read as voids. The facade is terminated by a missed beat (one window bay) a slight projection of the wall plane, a semi-baroque corner bay window and an extended parapet above eaves level.

Grecian Chambers

Ground floor shops, attached pylon aedicules to first floor windows, the intervening wall plane subsequently profiled to receive dwarf cylindrical tapered columns. The upper fenestration is apparently continuous but is in fact attached. The return elevation is flatter and can be compared with the elevation of Caledonia Road Church.

Egyptian Halls

An example of the 'suspended' facade made apparent through the inverse disposition of the columnar order, progressively heavier towards the cornice. The scrolls to the first floor level attached columns are reminiscent of a similar cast-iron detail in the Dixon Street Warehouse project. Continuous fenestration behind the columns appears at the upper floor.

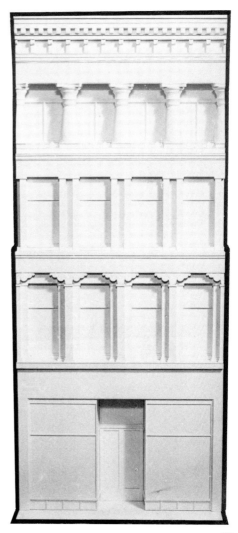

CAIRNEY BUILDING

An example of the tripartite division of the elevation consisting of ground floor shop, attached aedicules to first floor windows, stepped section over second floor windows with free-standing columns and continuous fenestration to the third floor. A fourth attic floor above cornice level is lit by a continuous rooflight.

CALEDONIA ROAD CHURCH

Thomson's first church commission: an asymmetric composition of symmetrical parts – church, tower and hall – placed to accommodate two converging street lines. The colonnaded clerestory screen had translucent glazing set directly between masonry. Entrances are denoted by the static pylon form and blank recessed panels (windows in an earlier scheme) on the side elevation. The long section illustrates Thomson's concern with light – a rooflight to the entrance hall and another to light the rear rows of seating are both set behind the main portico.

Thomson also designed the tenement immediately adjoining the church, the articulation of the stonework in each recognising the function of the public building as terminating a continuous street elevation. Comparison between Thomson's tenement and its neighbour lucidly illustrates the totality of composition of the former.

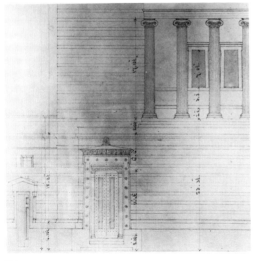

Robert McDougall
14 oct 1866

Double Villa

Two villas in one organised through rotational symmetry around a cross axis. Pairing two dwellings, each facing in opposite directions, creates the impression of one villa of a grander scale. The villa also features the detached fenestration which was to reappear in later buildings.

Drawing by Gerry Grams, David Fleming

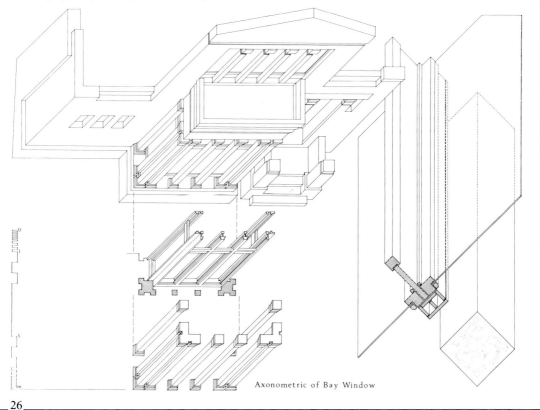

Axonometric of Bay Window

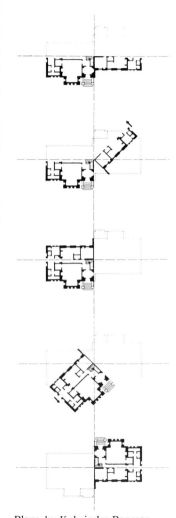

Plans by Kulwinder Panesar

Queen's Cross Tenements

A prime example of the imposition of a regular spacing of paired windows along a facade, the single windows a penultimate termination of the window rhythm. The partially colonnaded screen on the upper level implies continuous clerestory fenestration behind.

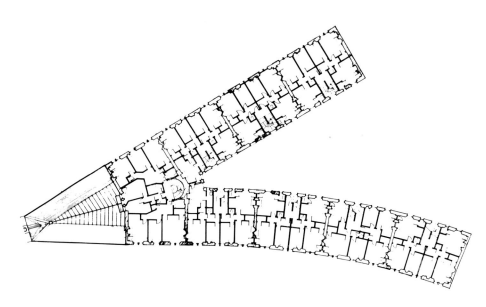

Drawing by Ian Miller

Dixon Street/Howard Street Warehouse *(Project)*

An early experiment with cast-iron. Thomson
rarely gave such pronounced recognition to
turning a corner.

A. Thomson, ST GEORGE'S CHURCH, Edinburgh.

Trabeated Essence and Frosted Glass[1]

John McKean

We have hitherto looked at the outsides of things . . .
Alexander Thomson

A great building, in my opinion, must begin with the unmeasurable, must go through measurable means when it is being designed and in the end must be unmeasurable. . . The only way you can build is through the measurable. You must follow the laws, but in the end when the building becomes part of living, it evokes unmeasurable qualities. The design involving quantities of brick, method of construction, engineering is over and the spirit of existence takes over.
Louis I. Kahn

The moulded stone profile directly confronts a plane of glass. There is no junction; no compromise of a window frame confuses the distinction. The stone form vanishes into the opaque glass. Inside the building, the same detail and impression are repeated in reverse. For although it cannot be perceived through the translucent but clouded pane, the profile of the wall moulding continues through the screen.

Whatever we are looking at, it is clearly not a 'window' in the tradition of being a hole in a wall. Rather the glass is a sealing layer, a plane within a trabeated system. A series of columns and lintels is infilled with glass; this sheet seals the envelope from the inclement Glaswegian weather, but in so doing it emphasises that it is an addition to the architecture itself. The stone detail is hard and sharp, the columns deep and, from most perspectives, the glass is lost in shadow. The clarity inside the building mirrors this: bright, even, white light between sharply profiled dark columns.

Concentrating briefly on Thomson's use of the wall and window, I want to suggest that he tried to avoid the 'measles' of the infectious stylistic revivals, as his contemporary Owen Jones called them, by aiming for timeless values; moreover that in concentrating on an ideal, via the abstract, he was using a history which was not developmental but rather transcendental, aiming to reveal essences.

As we draw back from such a close focus on this detail an architectural form is revealed which is not the distillation of a slow cultural development through two and a half thousand years of Western culture from its distant heritage. It has not learned from the evolving architectural forms of preceding centuries. Rather, it seems somehow to have been directly transplanted, plucked from the sharp sunlight of the ancient eastern Mediterranean. An idea of some Classical original is still very near the surface. Its appearance here, in bustling, canny, bourgeois Glasgow, is clearly polemical.

We are looking at what was the United Presbyterian Church on Caledonia Road, Glasgow; Alexander Thomson's first major building. When it was built (1856) direct glazing techniques were

K.F.Schinkel, ORIANDA PALACE. 'Most close to the spirit of Thomson.'

extremely rare;[2] but technical novelty is irrelevant. Thomson was not essentially concerned with developing or even expressing new materials or ideas.[3] He had a clear and remarkably uncompromised pictorial, and abstract, intention. Such technical originality as direct glazing was fortuitous –as it had been for so many others: such as Leo von Klenze's cast-iron roof on his Parthenon/Walhalla (1842), or Schinkel's projected palace for Tzarina Orianda in the Crimea (1838).

This Schinkel scheme is particularly interesting where its detail is most close to the spirit of Thomson – a pair of semi-circular bays flanking a portico on caryatids. Here glass is held between the columns as if in neoprene gaskets.[4] The parallel with Thomson, perhaps particularly to the porch in his sketch for St George's Church, Edinburgh (1858) which today hangs in the Mackintosh School of Architecture, is beyond coincidence. The column and architrave are the form, which contains the architectural intentions; the screen is only the 'necessary licence'[5] and it is as unobtrusive as possible. The technical solution, possible for Thomson in a way it couldn't have been so few years earlier for Schinkel, stems nevertheless from his stubborn thinking through of a pictorial problem.

This is seen even more clearly in the Double Villa (also 1856). From outside the edges are crisp. Stone profile abuts shadow, and stands out sharply against the grey between columns. In elevation the impression is the same as the detail with which I began; in Thomson's drawing it looks identical. The trabeated form here as always defines the space – precisely drawn in black ink, the stonework washed russet and the sharply cut gaps washed grey. In this case, however, the sealing curtain, instead of blocking the interstices, takes the form of a timber-framed glazed screen. The columns stand clear of the non-loadbearing glazing behind.

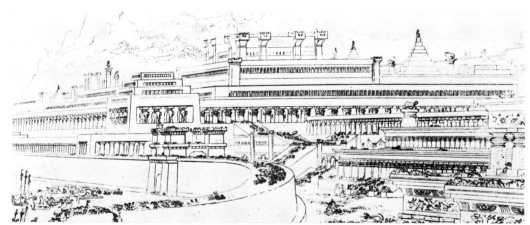

J. Martin, THE FALL OF NINEVEH. 'Martin's grandiose and ultimately banal architectural compositions.'

It has been called curtain-walling inside out; but of course it is nothing of the sort in intention. Rather it is a logical answer to Thomson's architectural *a priori*; and a taste which derives its neo-Classical origin ultimately from Laugier's *Essai*,[6] with its demand for expression of both the apparent and actual solidity of trabeated construction.

Following Laugier the window is excused as a 'licence'; in principle it is undesirable, if inevitable. But, just as principles are often taken up to suit a taste, so Thomson's 'Greek' rationalisations seem justifications of his natural preference. His image was based on a picturesque antiquity from the eastern Mediterranean. The adaptation of this vision to the condition of nineteenth-century urban Scotland was to be for him a major task.

It has been said that Thomson had a horror of openings. This is only part truth; it is clearly the compromise of window frames rather than openings themselves which he resisted. His ideal is the trabeated forms of Egypt or Greece. This alone, in its sharp outlines, its uncompromising junctions of solid and void, of light and dark, retains in execution the precision which he demanded. With a taste very akin to much of Modernism, he abhorred ambiguity, or any 'soft' junctions. He was antithetical to any flow of spaces round forms, to any baroque complexity.

Of course, he had not met windows in any antique architecture. They do not appear in Gardner Wilkinson's Egypt,[7] Fergusson's India,[8] Martin's Nineveh[9] or on the Athenian acropolis. Openings are formed by colonnades and colonnaded galleries.[10] Until the very end of his life (his final Great Western Terrace is a supreme exception) Thomson spent considerable effort and ingenuity in trying to disguise the fact that he was designing windows. In different forms, this preoccupation is clear in

A. Thomson, MORAY PLACE, Strathbungo.   Photo: T. Annan and Son

'The ideal way to eliminate the "window"; at party-walls blind bays are introduced, but in perspective these submerge the differentiation of the houses ...'

nearly all his work. 'It is only by a special favour that he tolerates doors or windows or even walls!' said Chambers, deriding the Abbé Laugier,[11] and this comment may equally apply to Thomson.

Lecturing at the end of his life, Thomson commented, during an attack on windows, that the death of architecture was heralded when architects – from Rome through the Middle Ages to the Renaissance – became more interested in voids than in solids. Windows, he added, could not be treated with the same subtlety as solids, whether planar masses or colonnades.

A. Thomson, EGYPTIAN HALLS.
'Piling layer on layer of outrageous colonnade.'

The ideal way to eliminate the image of 'window' is to incorporate it in a structural colonnade. In his first attempts this is clear; at Moray Place it becomes obvious. The two-storey colonnade, flanked by porticos, is based directly on the ancient *stoa*. The interstices are glazed – but not entirely, for inevitably at the party-walls between houses blank areas are necessary and blind bays are introduced in the same plane as the glass. In perspective, this submerges the rhythm of the individual house units. The metal window frames are hidden behind the stone columns; the top fixed lights

A. Thomson, SOUTH KENSINGTON MUSEUM Competition.

'"By some miracle of ingenuity, Hamilton managed to accommodate the school with hardly a single window showing in the grand front ...," Sir John Summerson said of the Edinburgh High School, one of Thomson's few acknowledged influences.'

directly glazed (as on the churches) and the opening lights below held as discreetly as possible.

The idea continued to haunt Thomson, but in no subsequent building was it ever as transparent. Where windows were unavoidable and yet a row of columns impractical, he tried to minimise them by focusing attention on something other than the window itself. Either he creates a pattern on the facade into which openings could be fitted unobtrusively, or he organises the window into a dominant frame.

A. Thomson, ST VINCENT STREET CHURCH.
'It is clearly not "window", but rather a sealing layer, a frosted plane within a trabeated image ...'

The latter theme, that of having objects in a showcase, well-modelled in three-dimensional contrast to the surrounding wall surface, is first seen in the caryatids on the tower of St Vincent Street church. It is used more clearly on the two projects, the Albert Memorial (1862) and the South Kensington Museum (1864), on which Thomson was working immediately prior to the design of Queen's Park Church (1867). In the later project, elephant caryatids are found close together in deep niches, 'supporting' the temple above but also hiding the ground floor windows[12] while in the earlier a long bank of light is united behind a row of hefty caryatid busts, similar to those on St Vincent Street church tower. Finally, a group of short, closely-spaced columns, thick and rounded are framed in a deep niche on the facade of Queen's Park Church. Externally they may express the heavy structure, the weight and the power; but they are primarily concealing necessary glazing.

Inevitably, there were other situations where even this device could not be used. The glazing could not be grouped, but must be regular. This was the controlling factor of the facades of the commercial blocks and, even more, of the tenement housing. Here, all Thomson's ingenuity in the manipulation of planes, slightly recessing and advancing them to create patterns and zig-zag features, came to be employed.

The top storeys of tenement blocks usually fought to hold an image of the colonnade, and this theme is again found on the warehouses, although handled rather differently. Here, epitomised in the Cairney Building,[13] Thomson's finest commercial block, the columns rise from between the aedicules of the lower window to become fully modelled and three-dimensional supports for the entablature and cornice. Behind this form, and completely detached, the glazing is a screen wall in timber frame, while higher, hidden from the street by the cornice, an attic floor is lit by a continuous sloping band of glass.

Thomson's architectonic expression of the problem of the window, and the closely related concern with the metaphor of structure, exemplify much of his intentions. His position is essentialist rather than historicist; he is aiming for an expression of the ideal rather than a clarification of the real. But that search for what we might call archetypal forms took him along slippery ground. For in trying to extract symbolic or meaningful form, he risked simply reifying particular fragments from history. Those 'eternal qualities', glimpsed in periods when 'the highest powers of the greatest minds were taxed to express in symbols and in abstract forms those ideas of beauty and grandeur',[14] were contained, the self-educated Thomson felt, in the ancient cultures of his taste – Egypt, Central America, Hindu and, his epitome, Classical Greece.

But his use of 'symbol' is sentimental and romantic. By extracting those fragments from their specific contexts, they are made to convey the abstracted reactions which his taste demands: grandeur, mystery or majesty. Inevitably cut off from their historic meanings, they are reified as 'symbolic', rather than rooted as symbols of a contingent reality.

So now we see the problems of his contemporaries, almost all of them associational historicists, are avoided; and how Protestant churches could happily accept heathen Hindu forms, how sober educative museums can resemble nothing so much as the fall of corrupt Nineveh.

How Thomson found a ready Glaswegian clientele for this position is a fascinating study; here there is only space to hint. Partly, perhaps, the Calvinist suspicion of ritual was a symbolic amnesia which, with nouveau bourgeois demand for pomp, prepared the United Presbyterian worshippers to accept Thomson's own iconography for what was almost its 'Presbyterian Judaism'.

Thus Queen's Park Church becomes more comprehensible than it was to the High Church Ford

A. Thomson, QUEEN'S PARK CHURCH.

'The Scottish dream recreation of Solomon's temple … The image stops just short of Cecil B. DeMille.'

Photo: National Buildings Record of Scotland

A. Thomson, QUEEN'S PARK CHURCH.

'No longer just necessary envelope, now a wall of light . . .'

Photo: National Buildings Record of Scotland

Maddox Brown, who asked for what religion it had been intended. The facade contains the Old Testament historical-religious vision; one might say the interior contains the Scottish dream recreation of Solomon's temple. It was a fascinating reification of that mixture of richness and austerity, of geometric purity and blazing polychromy,[15] of that exuberance and yet sombreness, which typified its congregation of puritanical merchant Whigs. The image stops just short of Cecil B. DeMille.

Concern with 'the essence or nature of a thing', as Thomson put it,[16] suggests an idealist split from the world of present reality. Certainly Thomson saw the search for a 'modern' architecture as his most serious task. And it is surely a strength to see style and novelty as equally inadequate definitions for a new architecture[17] – it is this which links him most closely to the essentialism of the early twentieth century.

But his aim was to throw all history into the crucible, reduce it to fluid thought, and distil its essence[18] – away from the contingent world. Such a cut-off position must have had obvious attraction amidst the reality of Glasgow in the fifties. The contrast of slums and mercantile wealth was shocking – Thomson after all, as a designer, was building tenements of 'single ends'. Moreover, cholera broke out in the city in 1854, when he had a vulnerable family of four children aged under five. Within three years, by the time he was forty, four of Thomson's by then five children were dead. To dream of a scheme of meanings based on eternal values was a more solid alternative to dabbling in fancy dress.

'The promoters of the Greek Revival failed, not because of the scantiness of the material but because they could not see through the material into the laws upon which architecture rested', he said.[19] To incorporate timeless values, however, rather than to adapt or adopt 'styles', meant in the end to make timeless buildings. And this was Thomson's impossibility: for no-one can pull themselves right away from the sticky surface of the contingent world.

In an era more self-conscious than ever before of the relationship between artefact and culture[20] and where 'modern delineators and photographers have enabled us to gather together examples of the achievements of all who have gone before us',[21] Thomson tried hard to loosen himself. 'If we are only watchful, the process, by being oft repeated, must lead to improvement and ultimate emancipation'.[22]

It was a desperate hope; and he was to build no more important works after issuing these cries. And yet it *is* obvious from his intentions, and also clear in the startling freedom and originality of the buildings, that Thomson was considerably successful in cutting himself loose from that cultural history which so encumbered him. But extracting himself from this context to position himself in the wider and more fundamental one, must have been finally self-defeating. For in its synthesis it ultimately depended on himself. It may have been less self-indulgent than the associationist principles he eschewed, but it remained personal rather than cultural, relying on personal criteria and a personal synthesis. His way had an inevitable dead end, although it was perhaps no less fascinating a dead end than that which produced the shining white new buildings of the nineteen twenties and thirties.

His recent biographer misses the point as profoundly as those earlier admirers who called him "Greek". For example: 'Thomson was on the threshold of breaking through into what could be described as a new, or modern, architecture . . . He seemed to be looking into the future, seeing a new architecture based on function . . .'[23] 'The way ahead to a new architecture based on function, and its expression by a simple use of structure and materials, lay wide open before him . . . He had forged his own style of modern architecture and stood looking into the future seeing a new architecture based on functions, structure (the recent 1851 Exhibition still fresh in his mind) and the elimination of extraneous ornament.'[24]

Such was far from Thomson's intention. Certainly his search was for a new architecture, but a basis of 'function' and 'structure', he might have said, would involve an unpardonable trivialisation of the legacy of Ictinus and Callicrates.

But we are not interested in Thomson's idealist intentions alone; what engages us is his battle to express them in built form. With Queen's Park Church, at the age of fifty, the ultimate position seems to have been reached and Thomson can extend himself no more. On the facade a huge horizontal hole is cut in the wall. Within this, four thick and bulging columns struggle to support the weight above. Deep behind the columns, the glazing is invisible. Almost identical to his unidentified drawing of a monument set in a threatening desert, the heavy masonry dome here epitomises mysterious weight and sombre solidity.

Once inside, however, the same space could hardly be more different and unexpected. The church is a box with gallery and clerestory. Very much as St Vincent Street, but without the portico, the internal back wall can now be pushed outwards and an upper gallery introduced, banking up to the screen of glass behind. The whole mass of masonry, which we know to be above, is visually rejected and elegantly supported on eight precariously slender iron columns. The impression is one of clarity and light.

At the beginning, I described the glass in his churches as an addition to this architecture, as a 'necessary licence'. This is transparent with the Schinkel example, but perhaps that is not the whole story with Thomson. Is there a clue in his use of frosted glass? Only a decade separates Caledonia Road Church, one of his first mature works, from Queen's Park Church, one of his last. But something important has changed. No longer is it built on an honest expression of the trabeated form. Now this row of columns is far more massive externally than structurally necessary; internally, and for utterly contradictory effect, the frosted glass denies the columns beyond. It is not now just the necessary envelope from the weather, behind a polemical facade. We have the wall of light, an architectonic element in its own right, and a masterly effect. Just with that use of frosted glass, our real world can reclaim this architecture from abstraction. Thomson is allowing the buildings to be both more rooted in reality and more formally inventive, to be more than simply a built version of a theory of trabeated essence.

Footnotes

1. This speculative fragment was presented at the Mackintosh School of Architecture in December 1983, and derives partly from my MA thesis (University of Essex, 1970).
2. A few years earlier, Thomson had made one of the first recorded British uses of such techniques; the first European example is dated 1849.
3. John Baird designed the technically advanced and subtly lithe Argyll Arcade in 1827 and Gardners' Warehouse in 1855, each a masterpiece in expression of the new technical possibilities. For twelve years between these designs, Thomson worked with Baird, becoming his chief assistant. It was twelve years in which very little of interest, and nothing approaching such inventiveness, came from the office.
4. The extent of Thomson's knowledge of Schinkel is uncertain. McFadzean lamely says: *The question of possible Schinkel influence on Thomson is a very debatable point but Thomson could have received just as much inspiration from the work of Leo von Klenze or, nearer home, from Thomas Hamilton and W.H. Playfair. The case for Schinkel remains unproven.* (*The Life and Work of Alexander Thomson*, London 1979, note 14, p.290.) Schinkel's *Sammlung Architectonischer Entwurfe* was published in parts from 1819-1840 and not as a bound folio volume until 1873. However the Crimean palace was not published until the coloured lithographs of the posthumous *Werken der Hoheren Baukunst*, Potsdam, 1840-1848.
5. The phrase of the Abbé Laugier, *Essai sur l'architecture*, 1752.
6. Abbé Laugier, *Essai sur l'architecture*, 1752.
7. J. Gardner Wilkinson, *The Architecture of Ancient Egypt*, 1850.
8. James Fergusson, *Ancient Architecture in Hindustan*, 1847, and his many other volumes.
9. John Martin, 'The Fall of Nineveh' engraving of 1828. Martin was one of the very few artists Thomson said he admired.
10. The pattern of holes punched in a plane is so rare that the west front of the Erectheion, where the window frames are between engaged columns, seems unique. This was a point remarked by Thomson in his third Haldane Lecture (*The British Architect* Vol.II, 1874, p.50).
11. William Chambers, *A Treatise on Civil Architecture*, 1759, p.58.
12. This detail is taken directly from a Martin engraving.
13. Bath Street, Glasgow. Demolished by Glasgow Corporation for tramway offices, early twentieth century.
14. Alexander Thomson, four lectures on art and architecture to the Glasgow School of Art and Haldane Academy, 1874. Lecture II, published in *The British Architect* Vol. I, pp.354-7.
15. With this, Thomson was aided by Daniel Cottier, who had been a pupil of Brown in London.
16. Thomson (as footnote 14), Lecture I, *The British Architect* Vol. I, pp.274-8.
17. See particularly his presidential address to the Glasgow Institute of Architects; reported in *The Glasgow Herald*, 8.4.1871.
18. He uses almost exactly these words in 'An enquiry into the appropriateness of Gothic ...' lecture, on 7.5.1866, *Proceedings of The Glasgow Architectural Society* 1865-7, pp.43-70 and ibid.
19. Thomson (as footnote 14), Lecture III, *The British Architect* Vol. II, pp.50-52, 82-84.
20. Cf. the booming interest in archaeology, or the work on geological dating by William 'Strata' Smith.
21. Thomson (as footnote 18).
22. Thomson (as footnote 17).
23. Ronald McFadzean, *The Life and Work of Alexander Thomson*, London 1979, pp.114, 283.
24. Ronald McFadzean, 'The Villas of Alexander Thomson', 1971 RIAS Prize Essay.

CHRONOLOGICAL LIST OF WORKS

It is impossible to compile a complete list of Thomson's works as many have been demolished before they could be recorded and, in other cases, the buildings survive but their authenticity cannot be confirmed.

It is also difficult to date accurately many of his buildings and designs. Consequently, the dates given should be regarded as being accurate within a tolerance of one or, in some cases, two years. In almost every case the date is the commencement of construction and not the design or completion.

1850
Seymour Lodge, Cove

Craig Ailey, Kilcreggan

Manhattan Cottage, 16 St Andrew's Drive, Pollokshields, Glasgow. Demolished 1964

Beech Villa, 18 St Andrew's Drive, Pollokshields, Glasgow. Demolished 1964

Green Gables, 20 St Andrew's Drive, Pollokshields, Glasgow. Demolished 1964

Lincoln Villa, 15 St Andrew's Drive, Pollokshields, Glasgow. Demolished 1965

Woodside Cottages, Langbank

1851
Ardsloy, Cove

Italian Villa, Cove

The Garnkirk Vase (for the 1851 Exhibition)

1852
The Knowe, 301 Albert Drive, Pollokshields, Glasgow (first stage)

Design for a Romanesque Church (*Mitchell Library Collection*)

1853
Warehouse at 36-38 Howard Street, Glasgow. Demolished 1966

1854
The Knowe, 301 Albert Drive, Pollokshields, Glasgow (second stage)

Rockland, Helensburgh, Dunbartonshire

Craigrownie Castle, Cove, Dunbartonshire (alterations and additions)

Knockderry Castle, Kilcreggan, Dunbartonshire (alterations and additions)

Schoolhouse, High Street, Glasgow. Demolished

1855
Gleneden Villa, Bothwell, Lanarkshire

Greenbank, Bothwell, Lanarkshire

Pollok School, 2097 Pollokshaws Road, Glasgow. Demolished 1968

The Knowe, 301 Albert Drive, Glasgow (third stage)

Scottish Exhibition Rooms, Bath Street, Glasgow. Demolished 1872

Tor House, Craigmore, Isle of Bute

1856
Balfron South Manse, Balfron, Stirlingshire

The Double Villa, Mansionhouse Road, Glasgow

Hutchesontown and Caledonia Road United Presbyterian Church, 1 Caledonia Road, Glasgow. Gutted 1965

Design for Warehouse in Howard Street, Glasgow (*Mitchell Library Collection*)

Design for Warehouse in Dixon Street, Glasgow (*Mitchell Library Collection*)

Busby House, Field Road, Busby, Lanarkshire (alterations and additions). Demolished 1969

Studio, Cathedral Street, Glasgow, for John Mossman. Destroyed 1875

1857
Holmwood, Netherlee Road, Cathcart, Glasgow

190-192 Hospital Street, Hutchesontown, Glasgow. Demolished 1973

37-39 Cathcart Road, Hutchesontown, Glasgow. Demolished 1968

Walmer Crescent, Paisley Road West, Ibrox, Glasgow

Queen's Park Terrace, 355-429 Eglinton Street, Glasgow

St Vincent Street United Presbyterian Church, 265 St Vincent Street, Glasgow

Design for unidentified house (*Mitchell Library Collection*)

1858

Monument, Glasgow Necropolis, A.O. Beattie

307 Eglinton Street/60 Cavendish Street, Laurieston, Glasgow. Demolished 1969

Design for St George's Church, Edinburgh (*Glasgow School of Art Collection*)

99-107 West Nile Street, Glasgow

164-178 St George's Road, Glasgow. Demolished 1970

1859

Chalmers Free Church, 42-50 Ballater Street, Glasgow. Gutted 1971

Washington Hotel, 126-32 (later 172) Sauchiehall Street, Glasgow. Demolished 1935

1-10 Moray Place, Strathbungo, Glasgow

3-11 Dunlop Street, Glasgow (date unconfirmed). Demolished 1973

1860

Tenement, 249-259 St Vincent Street, Glasgow. Demolished 1967

Cairney Building, Bath Street, Glasgow. Demolished *c.* 1935

Design for small church and manse (*Mitchell Library Collection*)

1861

Grosvenor Building, 68-80 Gordon Street, Glasgow. Fire Damage 1967

Tenement, 26-44 Norfolk Street, Glasgow. Demolished 1974

1862

Design for unidentified Monumental Building (*Mitchell Library Collection*)

Design for the Albert Memorial Competition (*Glasgow School of Art Collection*)

Obelisk for London Exhibition

1863

Buck's Head Building, 63 Argyle Street, Glasgow

Wall and gates at Ferndean Villa, Cove, Dunbartonshire

Left: TWO CHURCHES (*Projects*)
These two modest projects display all the formal and compositional devices of their larger counterparts.

1864

Langside Academy (date conjectural). Demolished

Design for South Kensington Museum Competition (*Mitchell Library Collection*)

Headstone, Balfron Churchyard, James Thomson

1865

Terrace at 27-53 Oakfield Avenue, Hillhead, Glasgow

Grecian Chambers, 336-56 Sauchiehall Street, Glasgow

1866

Northpark Terrace, 35-51 Hamilton Drive, Belmont, Glasgow

Unexecuted project for Glasgow Improvement Trust

1867

Queen's Park United Presbyterian Church, Langside Road, Glasgow. Destroyed 1943

Great Western Terrace, Great Western Road, Glasgow

Monument in Old Cathcart Cemetery, John McIntyre

1868

No recorded work

1869

Lilybank House, Hillhead, Glasgow (additions and alterations)

1870

National Bank, Union Street, Glasgow

Castlehill, 202 Nithsdale Road, Pollokshields, Glasgow

Design for Loch Katrine Monument Competition

1871

Ellisland, 200 Nithsdale Road, Pollokshields, Glasgow

Blackie's Printing Works, 17 Stanhope Street, Glasgow. Demolished 1967

The Egyptian Halls, 84-100 Union Street, Glasgow

Westbourne Terrace, 21-39 Hyndland Road, Kelvinside, Glasgow

1872

Stairway from Kelvinside Terrace West to Queen Margaret Road, Glasgow

Cowcaddens Cross Building, 110-120 Cowcaddens Street, Glasgow. Demolished 1971

UNIDENTIFIED VILLA (*Project*) This design, though of unknown location, displays characteristic asymmetry in the assembly of its parts with the extended garden wall drawing the lodge within the overall composition.

Chalmers Free Church, 42-50 Ballater Street, Glasgow (additions and alterations). Gutted 1971

J.E. Walker Stables, Bath Street, Glasgow (conversion work). Demolished 1875

J.E. Walker Stables, Smith (now Otago) Street, Glasgow. Demolished *c.* 1934

Offices, 107 West Regent Street, Glasgow (extensions)

1873

84-112 Nithsdale Road, Strathbungo, Glasgow

1874

Tenement, 94-106 Smith (now Otago) Street, Glasgow

Shore Road Bridge, Cove, Dunbartonshire

Customs House, Clyde Street, Glasgow (alterations)

Tenement, 32-68 Gorbals Street, 12-24 Norfolk Street, Glasgow. Demolished 1975

1875

Tenements, Queen's Cross, Glasgow

Office Building, 87-97 Bath Street, Glasgow. Demolished 1970

Tenement, 265-289 Allison Street, Glasgow

Tenement, 174-206 Gibson Street, Glasgow

Alexandra Hotel, 148 Bath Street, Glasgow (alterations and additions). Demolished 1973

Rysland (now Croyland), 202 Ayr Road, Newton Mearns, Renfrewshire

United Presbyterian Manse, Parkhall, Duntocher, Dunbartonshire. Destroyed 1941

Pettigrew & Stephens, Bath Street, Glasgow (alterations and additions). Demolished 1972

1876

2-38 Millbrae Crescent, Langside, Glasgow

Tenement, 18-76 Nithsdale Road, Pollokshields, Glasgow

Tenement, 471-475 Scotland Street, Glasgow. Demolished

Villa at 336 Albert Drive, Pollokshields, Glasgow

Reproduced by kind permission of Ronald McFadzean

Right: OBELISK (*Project*) Detail

BIBLIOGRAPHY

ARTICLES BY ALEXANDER THOMSON

'Masonry, and how it may be improved' *Glasgow Herald,* 23 February 1859

Address to GAS, *Glasgow Herald,* 22 October 1861

'A critical analysis of the Classic and Mediaeval styles showing to what an extent the aesthetic element was inherent in each' *Builder,* 9 May 1863, p.337 and *Glasgow Herald,* 4 May 1863

'The unsuitableness of the Gothic style to modern requirements' *Glasgow Herald,* 19 April 1864

'Architecture, its present state and future prospects' *Evening Citizen,* 25 October 1865

'An enquiry as to the appropriateness of the Gothic style for the proposed buildings for the University' *Builder,* 19 May 1866, pp.368-71

'The city improvement scheme' *Morning Journal,* 17 March 1868

'Obstacles and aids to architectural progress' *North British Daily Mail,* 17 March 1869

Address to Glasgow Institute of Architects, *Glasgow Herald,* 8 April 1871

The Haldane Academy Lectures in 'Art and architecture: a course of four lectures' *The British Architect,* 1874. Lecture I Vol.I, pp.274-8; Lecture II pp.354-7; Lecture III Vol.II, pp.50-2, 82-4; Lecture IV pp.272-4, 288-9, 317-18

ARTICLES ABOUT ALEXANDER THOMSON

J. Addison, 'Some aspects of Greek architecture: including a study of the neo-Grec style in Europe' *RIBA Journal,* 9 January 1932, pp.165-80

D. Barclay, 'Greek Thomson. I – His life and opinions' *Architectural Review* Vol.XV, May 1904, pp.183-94

J. M. M. Billing, 'Alexander "Greek" Thomson, a study of the recreation of a style' *RIAS Quarterly* No.62, 1939, pp.20-9

R. Blomfield, 'Greek Thomson. II – A critical note' *Architectural Review* Vol.XV, May 1904, pp.194-5

L. B. Budden, 'The work of Alexander Thomson' *Builder,* 31 December 1910, pp.815-19

A. T. Edwards, 'Alexander "Greek" Thomson' *Architect's and Builder's Journal,* 13 May 1914, pp.350-2

L. Ettlinger, 'A German architect's visit to England in 1826' *Architectural Review,* May 1945, pp.131-4

T. Gildard, 'Greek Thomson' *Proceedings of the Royal Philosophical Society of Glasgow* Vol.XIX, 30 January 1888, pp.191-210

T. Gildard, 'Greek Thomson' *Proceedings of the Royal Philosophical Society of Glasgow* Vol.XXVI, 3 December 1894, pp.99-107

H. S. Goodhart-Rendel, 'Rogue architects of the Victorian era' *RIBA Journal* Vol.LVI, 1949, pp.251-9

N. R. J. Johnson, 'Alexander Thomson, a study of the basic principles of his design' *RIAS Quarterly* No.43, September 1933, pp.29-38

G. Law, 'Greek Thomson' *Architectural Review,* May 1954, pp.307-16

G. Law, 'Colonnades and temples, Greek Thomson's style' *Glasgow Herald,* 8 June 1954

P. McNeill and D. Walker, 'Greek Thomson' *Glasgow Review,* Summer 1965

D. S. Paterson, 'Glasgow – and its buildings' *RIAS Quarterly,* 1951, pp.21-5, 29-32

W. J. Smith, 'Glasgow – art and architecture' *RIAS Quarterly,* May 1951, pp.11-13

W. J. Smith, 'Glasgow – "Greek" Thomson, Burnet and Mackintosh' *RIAS Quarterly,* August 1951, pp.56-60

D. Thomson, 'Greek Thomson' *Architect,* 19 November 1886, pp.292-3